W9-AUK-341

Common Core Language Arts Workouts Grade 7

AUTHOR: Linda Armstrong

EDITORS: Mary Dieterich and Sarah M. Anderson

PROOFREADER: Margaret Brown

COPYRIGHT © 2015 Mark Twain Media, Inc.

ISBN 978-1-62223-524-7

Printing No. CD-404227

Mark Twain Media, Inc., Publishers
Distributed by Carson-Dellosa Publishing LLC

Visit us at www.carsondellosa.com

Table of Contents
With Common Core State Standards Correlations

Table of Contents
With Common Core State Standards Correlations (cont.)

Table of Contents
With Common Core State Standards Correlations (cont.)

Table of Contents
With Common Core State Standards Correlations (cont.)

CCSS.ELA-Literacy.W.7.8: Gather relevant information from multiple print and digital sources, using search terms effectively; assess the credibility and accuracy of each source; and quote or paraphrase the data and conclusions of others while avoiding plagiarism and following a standard format for citation.

CCSS.ELA-Literacy.W.7.9: Draw evidence from literary or informational texts to support analysis, reflection, and research.

CCSS.ELA-Literacy.W.7.9a: Apply Grade 7 Reading Standards to literature (e.g., "Compare and contrast a fictional portrayal of a time, place, or character and a historical account of the same period as a means of understanding how authors of fiction use or alter history.").

CCSS.ELA-Literacy.W.7.9b: Apply Grade 7 Reading Standards to literary nonfiction (e.g. "Trace and evaluate the argument and specific claims in a text, assessing whether the reasoning is sound and the evidence is relevant and sufficient to support the claims.").

Table of Contents
With Common Core State Standards Correlations (cont.)

Table of Contents
With Common Core State Standards Correlations (cont.)

* Skills and understandings that are particularly likely to require continued attention in higher grades as they are applied to increasingly sophisticated writing and speaking are marked with an asterisk (*).

Common Core State Standards © Copyright 2010. National Governors Association Center for Best Practices and Council of Chief State School Officers. All rights reserved.
For more information about the Common Core State Standards, visit <www.corestandards.org>.

Introduction to the Teacher

The time has come to make our children's reading, writing, and speaking education more rigorous. The Common Core State Standards were developed for this purpose. They guide educators and parents by outlining the skills students are expected to master at each grade level. The bar has been set high, but with a little help, students can meet the challenge.

Common Core Language Arts Workouts, Grade 7 is designed to assist teachers and parents who are implementing the new requirements. It is filled with skills practice pages, critical-thinking tasks, and creative exercises that correspond to each standard for language arts.

Each day, students will work with a different grade-level-specific language arts skill. The brief exercises will challenge them to read, think, and speak with improved facility.

Every page contains at least one "workout." The workouts vary according to the standard covered. Some are simple practice exercises. Others pose creative or analytical challenges. Certain pages invite further exploration. Suggested student projects include reports, speeches, discussions, and multimedia presentations.

The workout pages make great warm-up or assessment exercises. They can set the stage and teach the content covered by the standards. They can also be used to assess what students have learned after the content has been taught.

We hope that the ideas and exercises in this book will help you work more effectively with the Common Core State Standards. The series also includes books for Grade 6 and Grade 8. With your help, we are confident that students will develop increased language arts power and become more effective communicators!

Name: _____ Date: _____

READING LITERATURE – Story Elements and Inferences

CCSS.ELA-Literacy.RL.7.1: Cite several pieces of textual evidence to support analysis of what the text says explicitly as well as inferences drawn from the text.
CCSS.ELA-Literacy.RL.7.2: Determine a theme or central idea of a text and analyze its development over the course of the text; provide an objective summary of the text.
CCSS.ELA-Literacy.RL.7.3: Analyze how particular elements of a story or drama interact (e.g., how setting shapes the characters or plot).

Directions: Read the selection. Answer the questions.

Deliberate footsteps echoed in the stone corridor. They were approaching rapidly. Desperately, Sophia sought a place to conceal the talisman William had entrusted to her. The high-ceilinged room, lit by a solitary arched window, contained little furniture. A pair of heavy carved chairs sat astride a small chest.

A smaller chair sat before the loom which held her sister's half-finished tapestry. Below the wooden frame, on the floor, sat a basket filled with skeins of colorful silk yarn.

The chest was too obvious. They would look there first. The footsteps stopped. The guards were just outside. Sophia slipped the brooch with its mysterious golden stone into the yarn basket just as one of the guards banged on the heavy oak door.

Commanding herself to remain calm, she settled into the chair in front of the loom and picked up a skein of blue silk.

She took a deep breath to steady herself. "What is it?" she asked.

1. What was the talisman? How do you know? _____

    _____

    _____

2. Were the people coming down the hallway probably friends or enemies?
    How do you know? _____

    _____

    _____

3. Was William a friend or an enemy? How do you know? _____

    _____

    _____

4. Does this story take place in the past, the present, or the future? How do you know?

    _____

    _____

    _____

Name: _____ Date: _____

READING LITERATURE – Analyzing a Poem

CCSS.ELA-Literacy.RL.7.4: Determine the meaning of words and phrases as they are used in a text, including figurative and connotative meanings; analyze the impact of rhymes and other repetitions of sounds (e.g., alliteration) on a specific verse or stanza of a poem or section of a story or drama.

Directions: Read the following poem. Answer the questions.

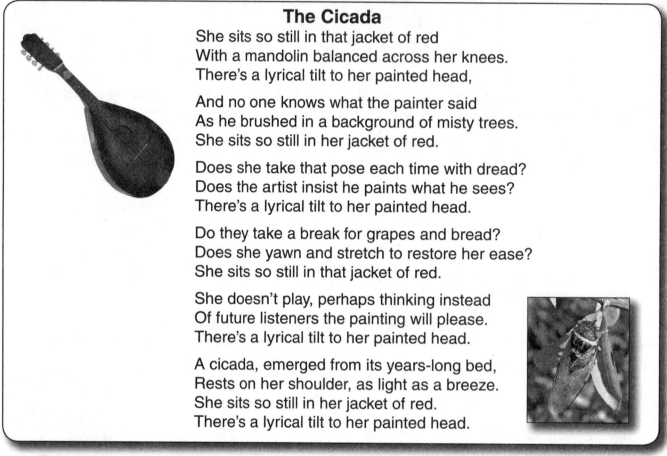

The Cicada

She sits so still in that jacket of red
With a mandolin balanced across her knees.
There's a lyrical tilt to her painted head,

And no one knows what the painter said
As he brushed in a background of misty trees.
She sits so still in her jacket of red.

Does she take that pose each time with dread?
Does the artist insist he paints what he sees?
There's a lyrical tilt to her painted head.

Do they take a break for grapes and bread?
Does she yawn and stretch to restore her ease?
She sits so still in that jacket of red.

She doesn't play, perhaps thinking instead
Of future listeners the painting will please.
There's a lyrical tilt to her painted head.

A cicada, emerged from its years-long bed,
Rests on her shoulder, as light as a breeze.
She sits so still in her jacket of red.
There's a lyrical tilt to her painted head.

1. This villanelle describes a painting by Jean-Baptiste Camille Corot. From clues provided in the poem, what does the painting depict? _____
   _____

2. Which four words in the poem relate to music or something that creates sound?
   _____

3. Which two lines are repeated in the poem? Which one talks about the model? Which one talks about the painting? How does their repetition add to the meaning of the poem?
   _____
   _____
   _____

4. What is a cicada? How is it related to the poem? _____
   _____

Name: _____ Date: _____

READING LITERATURE – Analyzing a Poem's Structure: The Sonnet

CCSS.ELA-Literacy.RL.7.5: Analyze how a drama's or poem's form or structure (e.g., soliloquy, sonnet) contributes to its meaning

Directions: Read the following sample sonnet. Answer the questions.

On Writing Sonnets

When writing sonnets, poets count each beat.
Ta dah, te boom, sha bam, te dah, sha boom.
They parcel out each line with measured feet.
They weave their rhythms on a vacant loom.

When crafting sonnets, poets choose each rhyme.
The weft shifts left, the warp is still. The frame
Is form. It holds the threads of thought in time.
The end of every other line will name

A dip or lift, idea born or lost
Emerging from this textile grown far past
Expected lengths of woven words to cost
A preconception all its force. At last,

In two short lines, the weaver ties up all;
A finished tapestry in poetry's hall.

1. What does this sonnet's form contribute to its meaning? _____
   _____

2. An *iamb* is a poetic foot. (tah <u>DAH</u>) How many iambs are there in each line of this verse? (Hint: see line 2) _____

3. A *quatrain* is a four-line stanza. How many quatrains are there in this Shakespearean sonnet? _____

4. A two-line poem or stanza is a *couplet*. Where is the couplet in this sonnet?
   _____

5. In this poem, writing a sonnet is compared with another activity. What is it? Is this kind of comparison a simile or a metaphor? Why? _____
   _____

6. What does *textile* mean? Why does it have an unusual meaning in this context?
   _____
   _____

Challenge: Print out a Shakespearean sonnet you find online. Mark the quatrains, rhymes, and iambs. What do you notice about the couplet?

Name: _____ Date: _____

READING LITERATURE – Points of View: A Sample Play

CCSS.ELA-Literacy.RL.7.6: Analyze how an author develops and contrasts the points of view of different characters or narrators in a text.

CCSS.ELA-Literacy.RL.7.7: Compare and contrast a written story, drama, or poem to its audio, filmed, staged, or multimedia version, analyzing the effects of techniques unique to each medium (e.g., lighting, sound, color, or camera focus and angles in a film).

Directions: Read the following scene. Answer the questions.

> *It is night in a forest clearing near Legend Lake Summer Camp. ABBY and SARAH enter.*
>
> ABBY: Shh! I hear someone coming.
>
> SARAH: You and your imagination. I don't know why I brought you along.
>
> ABBY: I'm just persuasive, I guess.
>
> SARAH: There's nothing out there, Abby, just trees and bushes.
>
> ABBY: Well, there isn't now, but there was.
>
> SARAH: Whatever. Just help me find my phone. If I don't call Mom tonight, she'll turn off my service.
>
> *SARAH and ABBY look for the phone on the ground under the trees. JACOB and RYAN enter. The girls do not see them.*
>
> JACOB: We've been wandering around for an hour and we haven't even seen a mouse. Let's go back to camp. I'm famished.
>
> RYAN: On wildlife observation missions, patience is mandatory.

Answer the questions on your own paper.

1. Which character is frightened? Which one is hungry? Which one is scientific? Which one is social? How do you know?
2. Act out the play with friends. How is it different from the written version?
3. Write a paragraph comparing a poem, book, or story you have read to its film or television adaptation. How did the filmmaker use music, lighting, camera angles, and special effects to make the story more powerful?

Challenge: Read the beginning of "The Invisible Man" by H.G. Wells. <http://www.gutenberg.org/files/5230/5230-h/5230-h.htm> Watch the beginning of one of the film versions. How are they different? How does the filmmaker set the mood?

Name: _____ Date: _____

READING LITERATURE – Fiction vs. Nonfiction

CCSS.ELA-Literacy.RL.7.9: Compare and contrast a fictional portrayal of a time, place, or character and a historical account of the same period as a means of understanding how authors of fiction use or alter history.

Directions: Read the following selections. Answer the questions.

> **Nonfiction:**
> The Great Depression was a period of severe hardship all over the world. It began with the crash of the stock market on Black Tuesday, October 29, 1929. The effects were devastating. More than 5,000 banks failed. Businesses cut back on orders, causing thousands of people to lose their jobs. More than a quarter of working adults were unemployed.
>
> **Fiction:**
> "But Ma, I don't want to live with Aunt Kate," Joe said.
> "Keep your voice down," his mother said, glancing into the living room. Pa hadn't moved. Perhaps he was asleep.
> "Your father feels bad enough. This is simply a matter of necessity," she said.
> Joe nodded. He didn't want to antagonize her, and it was useless to resist the inevitable.
> "Now go pack," Ma said. "We're leaving at sunup."

1. What does the nonfiction selection include that is not covered in the fiction selection?

   _____

   _____

2. What does the fiction selection include that is not covered in the nonfiction selection?

   _____

   _____

3. Why is it easier for fiction writers to use dialogue? What does it add to a text?

   _____

   _____

Challenge: Read "The Midnight Ride of Paul Revere" by Henry Wadsworth Longfellow at <http://www.poets.org/poetsorg/poem/paul-reveres-ride>, a letter describing the ride by Paul Revere himself at <http://www.masshist.org/database/viewer.php?item_id=99&img_step=1& mode=transcript#page1>, and a short nonfiction account of the event at The Paul Revere House <http://www.paulreverehouse.org/ride/real.html>.

Answer these questions on your own paper:
1. What facts does Longfellow change in his poem?
2. Why do you think more people remember the poem than the actual events of that night?
3. Why is this an important story in American history?

Name: _____ Date: _____

READING INFORMATIONAL TEXT – Textual Evidence and Central Ideas

CCSS.ELA-Literacy.RI.7.1: Cite several pieces of textual evidence to support analysis of what the text says explicitly as well as inferences drawn from the text.
CCSS.ELA-Literacy.RI.7.2: Determine two or more central ideas in a text and analyze their development over the course of the text; provide an objective summary of the text.

Directions: Read the following selection. Answer the questions.

Early Warning in Hawaii

It was seven in the morning on December 7. Private George E. Elliott, Junior and Private Third Class Specialist Joseph L. Lockhart were exhausted after their latest three-hour shift, but they decided to remain a little longer.

Private Elliott wanted an opportunity to practice using the monitoring equipment. He slid into the seat in front of the new SCR – 270 B Radio Direction Finder.

Suddenly, a mysterious blip appeared on the oscilloscope. When the peculiar signal persisted, the two observers in their trailer on Kahuku Point on Oahu called the Information Center at Fort Shafter.

Unfortunately, the officer on duty at the Center did not take their report seriously. If he had listened, the story of Pearl Harbor might have been different.

1. What job did Privates Elliott and Lockhart have? Which details in the text let you know?

_____

2 Which man was probably new on the job? What makes you think so?

_____

3. What is an oscilloscope? What is a blip? Use a dictionary to confirm your guess.

_____

_____

4. What year do you think this happened? What makes you think so?

_____

5. What do you think happened next? What makes you think so?

_____

_____

Challenge: Online or in a textbook, read an account of the attack on Pearl Harbor. On your own paper, summarize the selection in a paragraph or two. State at least two central ideas along with supporting details. Does the author of the article have any opinion about the cause of the attack or its results? If so, what was it? Include a quotation or details from the text to support your answer.

Name: _____ Date: _____

READING INFORMATIONAL TEXT – Ideas, Individuals, and Influences

CCSS.ELA-Literacy.RI.7.3: Analyze the interactions between individuals, events, and ideas in a text (e.g., how ideas influence individuals or events, or how individuals influence ideas or events).

Directions: Read the following selection and answer the questions.

Hannibal, Never a Friend to Rome

In the mid third century B.C., Rome and Carthage were rivals. Centered in North Africa, Carthage was a naval power. Its ships dominated the western Mediterranean. Rome did not have many ships. But its network of alliances was strengthening.

In 264 B.C., mounting tensions between the two powers led to war. Carthage was defeated. Its fighting ships were ruined, and Rome acquired Sicily.

Carthage needed resources. Hannibal's father, Hamilcar, readied his army to invade Hispania. Hannibal, then only nine, begged to go. Before leaving Carthage, Hamilcar took him to a temple. He made the boy vow never to befriend the Romans.

In 218 B.C., long after his father's death, Hannibal saw an opportunity to attack Rome. He gathered an unprecedented force. There were thousands of foot soldiers, horsemen, and even a troop of war elephants.

They crossed two formidable mountain ranges, the Pyrenees and the Alps. Though he lost much of his army on the trip, Hannibal almost succeeded. When he arrived in northern Italy, he surprised the Romans. With the help of unhappy northern Italian tribes, he won several battles. Unfortunately, he did not have the strength to attack the city of Rome.

Although, ultimately, Carthage lost the war, Hannibal is regarded as one of the greatest strategists in military history.

Answer these questions on another sheet of paper.

1. How did the loss of Sicily and the Carthaginian fleet affect Hamilcar?
2. How did Hannibal's vow to his father affect his decision to attack Rome?
3. How did the difficulty of crossing the Alps affect the outcome of Hannibal's campaign?

Challenge: Read an article about the Third Punic War online. What happened to Carthage? How might the world have been different if Hannibal had captured Rome?

Name: _____ Date: _____

READING INFORMATIONAL TEXT – Using Context Clues

CCSS.ELA-Literacy.RI.7.4: Determine the meaning of words and phrases as they are used in a text, including figurative, connotative, and technical meanings; analyze the impact of a specific word choice on meaning and tone.

Directions: Read the following selection. Answer the questions.

The Spirit of St. Louis

In 1919, New York hotel owner Raymond Orteig offered a provocative challenge. He would pay $25,000 to the first pilot who made a nonstop flight between New York and Paris.

Flying machines were still relatively new and undependable in the years following World War I. Six fliers lost their lives preparing for an attempt to win Orteig's prize. Then a handsome young aviator named Charles Lindbergh made a bid.

With backing from Harry H. Knight, Harold M. Bixby, and Frank Robertson, he had a monoplane constructed. They dubbed it *The Spirit of St. Louis.* Lindbergh took off on May 20, 1927. His solo flight lasted $33\frac{1}{2}$ hours.

His daring feat made Charles Lindbergh the most celebrated man in the world. It also made the planet smaller.

1. In what way was the planet "smaller" after Lindbergh's flight? _____
_____

_____

2. What does *nonstop* mean? _____

3. What does *undependable* mean? _____

4. What does *monoplane* mean? _____

5. What does *backing* mean in this text? _____

6. What does *fliers* mean in this text? Which word in the text is a synonym? _____
_____

7. What does *celebrated* mean in this text? _____

8. Which word in the text is a synonym for *attempt*? _____

9. What does *provocative* mean in this text? _____

10. The terms *flying machines, fliers,* and *aviator* are used in this selection. Which modern synonyms could have been used? Why do you think the author selected these outdated words instead?

_____

_____

Name: _____ Date: _____

READING INFORMATIONAL TEXT – All About Text Structure

CCSS.ELA-Literacy.RI.7.5: Analyze the structure an author uses to organize a text, including how the major sections contribute to the whole and to the development of the ideas.

Directions: Read the following selection and answer the questions.

Using Text Structure to Improve Comprehension

Types of Text Structures

Many nonfiction articles and books are arranged using text structures.

The description structure enumerates the characteristics of a person, place, or event. The comparison structure compares two or more items or concepts. The problem and solution structure lays out a problem, along with steps taken to resolve it, while the cause and effect structure juxtaposes actions and their aftermaths. The sequence structure, common in history and biographical texts, emphasizes the chronological order of events.

1. Circle the headings that would not fit additional sections of this article.

   A. Differentiating Fact From Opinion

   B. Text Structure Signal Words

   C. 10 Popular Authors

   D. Text Structure Examples

   E. How Text Structure Improves Comprehension

   F. The Importance of Setting in Fiction

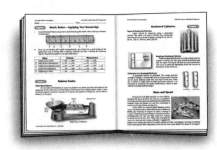

2. Explain your choices. _____

   _____

3. What is the heading of the sample section? _____

   _____

4. How do headings make an article easier to read? _____

   _____

5. Which text structure does the sample article follow? _____

Challenge: Examine a chapter from a geography, history, or science book. How could organizational signposts such as headings and text structure signal words help you to gather information or study for a test?

Name: _____ Date: _____

READING INFORMATIONAL TEXT – Finding the Author's Point of View and the Author's Purpose

CCSS.ELA-Literacy.RI.7.6: Determine an author's point of view or purpose in a text and analyze how the author distinguishes his or her position from that of others.

Directions: Follow the instructions in each section.

1. Circle the author's point of view for each type of text.
   a. a biography   first person   second person   third person
   b. an autobiography   first person   second person   third person
   c. interview questions   first person   second person   third person
   d. a chapter in a history text first person   second person   third person
   e. a diary or journal   first person   second person   third person

2. Explain the difference between the first-person and the third-person point of view.

   _____

   _____

3. Circle the author's purpose for each type of text.
   a. A book about the causes of World War II.   entertain   persuade   inform
   b. An automobile advertisement in a magazine.   entertain   persuade   inform
   c. A novel about a star quarterback   entertain   persuade   inform
   d. A weather forecast in the local newspaper.   entertain   persuade   inform

4. In what ways would an article about how to study differ from an article about why studying
   is important? _____

   _____

5. Read the following selection. Answer the questions.

   > Many people believe that Henry Ford invented the modern automobile. However, that is not the case. Actually, most authorities agree that the credit belongs to the German inventor, Karl Benz. He received a patent for his *Motorwagen* in 1886.

   a. The selection is written from what point of view? _____

   b. What is the author's purpose? _____

   c. Which two phrases does the author use to distinguish her position from that of others?

   _____   _____

Challenge: **CCSS.ELA-Literacy.RI.7.7:** Compare and contrast a text to an audio, video, or multimedia version of the text, analyzing each medium's portrayal of the subject (e.g., how the delivery of a speech affects the impact of the words).

a. Listen to Franklin Delano Roosevelt's speech "Americanism" on the American Memory site <memory.loc.gov>. Then read the text of the speech.
b. What is the speaker's purpose and point of view?
c. How does the experience of listening to the speech differ from the experience of reading it?

Name: _____ Date: _____

READING INFORMATIONAL TEXT – Believe It or Not?
Evaluating Claims

CCSS.ELA-Literacy.RI.7.8: Trace and evaluate the argument and specific claims in a text, assessing whether the reasoning is sound and the evidence is relevant and sufficient to support the claims.
CCSS.ELA-Literacy.RI.7.9: Analyze how two or more authors writing about the same topic shape their presentations of key information by emphasizing different evidence or advancing different interpretations of facts.

Directions: Read the selection. Answer the questions.

The Injustices of School
by
A. Poor Student

Some people characterize me as belligerent when I suggest that students are being bamboozled by academic expectations.

First, the advantage of being punctual is highly overemphasized. Dawdling in the morning is absolutely essential, especially after a televised football game runs late the previous night.

Second, I am constantly perplexed when teachers harass me for not completing assignments on time. Life is long, and there's always so much to do.

Third, grades are unfair. My parents are often irate when they receive my report card. This is a formidable stumbling block for my social life, especially when, as a result of my poor marks, I am grounded.

1. Which three academic expectations disturb the writer of this essay?

   a. _____ b. _____ c. _____

2. a. What reason does the writer offer for objecting to the first expectation? _____

   _____

   b. Is this a legitimate reason? _____

   c. Why or why not? _____

   _____

3. Do you think this article is meant to be serious or humorous? _____

   Give a reason for your answer. _____

   _____

Challenge: Online or in a newspaper, read and analyze an opinion article. On your own paper, name the writer's central point or points. What facts does the writer offer to support his or her ideas? Were his or her examples convincing? Why or why not?

WRITING—SECTION THEME: WRITING OPINION PIECES

CCSS.ELA-Literacy.W.7.1: Write arguments to support claims with clear reasons and relevant evidence.

Writing an Opinion

CCSS.ELA-Literacy.W.7.1a: Introduce claim(s), acknowledge alternate or opposing claims, and organize the reasons and evidence logically.
CCSS.ELA-Literacy.W.7.1b: Support claim(s) with logical reasoning and relevant evidence, using accurate, credible sources and demonstrating an understanding of the topic or text.

Directions: Read the following statement:

Some people think boys and girls should attend separate high schools. Do you agree or disagree?

Follow the instructions.

1. State your opinion in a sentence. _____

_____

_____

2. Give one reason for your opinion. _____

_____

_____

3. Offer one example supporting your opinion. _____

_____

_____

4. Explain the argument of those who disagree. _____

_____

_____

5. Write a concluding sentence, summarizing your opinion and your reasons for it.

_____

_____

_____

Challenge: Where could you find expert quotations, facts, or statistics to support your ideas? On your own paper, expand this paragraph into a short essay by including additional information.

Name: _____   Date: _____

WRITING OPINION PIECES – Clarifying Relationships With Connecting Words and Phrases

CCSS.ELA-Literacy.W.7.1c: Use words, phrases, and clauses to create cohesion and clarify the relationships among claim(s), reasons, and evidence.

Directions: Write one of the phrases from the box in each blank to connect the ideas.

in order to	during	consequently	similarly
on the other hand	as opposed to	not only – but also	following
to solve this	dilemma is	for instance	characteristic
to begin with	finally		

1. _____ the earthquake, a tsunami headed for the island. _____ authorities ordered an evacuation.

2. The coal-fired power plant closed. Now, the _____ whether to construct a solar or geothermal facility.

3. Insomnia is _____ unpleasant _____ dangerous.

4. Children were dying of polio. _____ problem, Jonas Salk developed a vaccine.

5. One _____ of iron pyrite (fool's gold) is its distinctive cubic crystal structure.

6. On the one hand, coal is abundant and inexpensive, while _____ it generates pollution.

7. _____ evergreen conifers, broadleaved deciduous trees lose their leaves in the winter.

8. Prospective team members had to agree to follow the group's rules. _____, they pledged to be punctual.

9. _____ protest the treatment of Rosa Parks, African-Americans organized a bus boycott.

10. After five years of fighting, a peace treaty was _____ negotiated.

11. _____ World War II, the U.S. forces established a liaison with Great Britain.

12. The earth orbits the sun and, _____, the moon orbits the earth.

Challenge: On your own paper, write a short original essay using at least four of the connecting phrases listed above.

Name: _____ Date: _____

WRITING OPINION PIECES – Make It Formal

CCSS.ELA-Literacy.W.7.1d: Establish and maintain a formal style.

Directions: Rewrite each sentence using a formal style. Use words from the box wherever possible.

convincing	qualified	for the most part		accounts	predict
factual	delivered	refused	competent	prominent	additional
consecutive	acquired	vital	irate	inhabitants	address
inaccuracies	famous	manner	chronologically	uninformed	events
bold move	rumors	consult	expeditions	yield	citizen
emphasize	information				

1. The writer was mad, and his article was filled with stuff that wasn't true.

   _____

2. Things were listed by when they happened.

   _____

3. An important guy in our town tried to make us back down, but we didn't.

   _____

4. The things folks in town said were just plain stupid.

   _____

5. The Senator served four terms, one after the other.

   _____

6. The astronaut was real well known for his true stories about his trips into space and stuff.

   _____

   _____

7. Nobody could tell from his expressions or anything what he was going to do.

   _____

8. Let me tell you, this stuff is really important.

   _____

9. The handyman is good enough to take care of easy wiring problems, but we should check with a real electrician before we do anything else.

   _____

   _____

10. Franklin Roosevelt gave a talk that made people believe him.

    _____

Challenge: On your own paper, use at least five of the words or phrases listed above in an original formal essay.

Name: _____ Date: _____

WRITING OPINION PIECES – Writing Conclusions

CCSS.ELA-Literacy.W.7.1e: Provide a concluding statement or section that follows from and supports the argument presented.

Directions: Write concluding statements for paragraphs presenting a set of ideas.

1. a. Counselors have years of training.
    b. Counselors want to help students.
    c. Counselors are good listeners.
    d. Counselors can help students succeed.

    _____

    _____

2. a. The Revolutionary War had many causes.
    b. Great Britain needed money.
    c. Great Britain raised taxes on things people in the Colonies needed.
    d. People in the colonies were used to making their own decisions.

    _____

    _____

3. a. Silicon is an element.
    b. Silicon is the second most common element in the earth's crust.
    c. At least 90% of the minerals in the earth's crust contain silicon.
    d. On Earth, only oxygen is more common than silicon.

    _____

    _____

4. a. Smoking is a health hazard.
    b. Smoking contributes to the development of lung cancer.
    c. Smoking contributes to heart disease.
    d. Secondhand smoke harms non-smokers.

    _____

    _____

5. a. There are five categories of hurricanes, according to the Saffir-Simpson Hurricane Wind Scale.
    b. Category one hurricanes have sustained wind speeds up to 95 miles per hour.
    c. Category three hurricanes have sustained wind speeds up to 110 miles per hour.
    d. The strongest hurricanes are category five, with winds in excess of 157 miles per hour.

    _____

    _____

Challenge: On your own paper, rewrite one of these sets of facts as a paragraph. Use transitional phrases and a formal style.

WRITING—SECTION THEME: WRITING INFORMATIVE AND EXPLANATORY TEXTS

CCSS.ELA-Literacy.W.7.2: Write informative/explanatory texts to examine a topic and convey ideas, concepts, and information through the selection, organization, and analysis of relevant content.

Conveying Ideas and Information

CCSS.ELA-Literacy.W.7.2a: Introduce a topic clearly, previewing what is to follow; organize ideas, concepts, and information, using strategies such as definition, classification, comparison/contrast, and cause/effect; include formatting (e.g., headings), graphics (e.g., charts, tables), and multimedia when useful to aiding comprehension.

Directions: Write a sentence for each purpose. Include the sample opening phrase or write your own.

1. Define *amendment*. _____

2. Classify the right to exercise religion, the right to free speech, and the right to freedom from search and seizure. *The rights to exercise religion, to free speech, and to freedom from search and seizure are all part of* _____

   _____

3. Compare *rights* and *privileges*. *Rights differ from privileges because* _____

   _____

4. State the general effect of the Bill of Rights. *Because of the Bill of Rights,* _____

   _____

   _____

5. Write a short paragraph including these four sentences, along with an introduction, transitional words or phrases, and a conclusion.

   _____

   _____

   _____

   _____

   _____

   _____

   _____

Challenge: On your own paper, write a brief report about the Bill of Rights. Include headings, quotations from experts, relevant anecdotes, and graphics. Include a list of your sources.

Name: _____ Date: _____

WRITING INFORMATIVE AND EXPLANATORY TEXTS – Using Facts, Definitions, Details, and Quotations

CCSS.ELA-Literacy.W.7.2b: Develop the topic with relevant facts, definitions, concrete details, quotations, or other information and examples.

Directions: Write four paragraphs on another piece of paper. Title them as follows: *Aquifers, The Benefits of Physical Activity, Deserts,* and *Hail.* In each paragraph use one fact, one definition, one detail, and one quotation from the chart below.

Facts	Definitions	Details	Quotations
The large deserts of the world occur near the Tropic of Cancer and the Tropic of Capricorn.	*aquifer:* an underground layer of sand or rock saturated with water	Regular activity benefits and improves concentration.	"Sunshine all the time makes a desert." Arab proverb
In 2013, only 27.1% of high school students participated in at least 60 minutes of activity during the week before a CDC survey.	*habitat:* the home of a group of specific plants and animals	Some hailstones are more than 4 inches across and weigh more than a pound.	"When the well is dry, we know the worth of water." Benjamin Franklin 1746
Different aquifers have different characteristics.	*CDC:* United States Centers for Disease Control and Prevention	Desert temperatures are extreme, with days reaching in excess of 122°F and nights falling as low as -4°.	"I wield the flail of the lashing hail, and whiten the green plains under, and then again I dissolve it in rain, and laugh as I pass in thunder." Percy Bysshe Shelley, "The Cloud"
Chunks of ice form in cumulonimbus clouds during thunderstorms.	*cumulonimbus:* storm clouds	Underground water moves slowly downhill, emerging in springs or wells.	"So your desire is to do nothing? Well, you shall not have a week, a day, an hour, free from oppression." Victor Hugo, *Les Miserables*

Challenge: Create a chart like this one to record information you plan to use in an essay or report. (This kind of form can also be used to record notes from a text or presentation.)

Name: _____ Date: _____

WRITING INFORMATIVE AND EXPLANATORY TEXTS – Using Transitions

CCSS.ELA-Literacy.W.7.2c: Use appropriate transitions to create cohesion and clarify the relationships among ideas and concepts.

Directions: Write the best transition word or phrase from the box in each space.

one may conclude that	first	as well as	the difference between
as opposed to	nevertheless	therefore	for this reason
in like manner	the loss	previously	the best estimate

1. Since the town's history is written in chronological order, _____ the earliest story appears at the beginning.

2. _____ our neighbor had always put out the trash on time, but that particular Tuesday, she forgot.

3. A predator is the hunter, _____ the prey, which is hunted.

4. Consumer organisms cannot create their own food, _____ they eat other plants and animals.

5. Evergreen trees, _____ corn plants and mosses, are producers, meaning they create energy-rich food molecules utilizing energy from the sun.

6. Use each phrase in a sentence.

   a. the difference between _____

   _____

   b. in like manner _____

   _____

   c. first _____

   _____

   d. therefore _____

   _____

   e. nevertheless _____

   _____

Challenge: On your own paper, revise a recent essay or report, adding appropriate transition words to connect ideas.

Name: _____   Date: _____

WRITING INFORMATIVE AND EXPLANATORY TEXTS –
Applying Technical Terminology

CCSS.ELA-Literacy.W.7.2d: Use precise language and domain-specific vocabulary to inform about or explain the topic.
CCSS.ELA-Literacy.W.7.2e: Establish and maintain a formal style.

Directions: Write the best word from the box on the line in each sentence. Use a dictionary if you are not sure.

acid	inclined plane	organelles	element	respiratory system
dissolves	cell membranes	friction	kinetic energy	tornado warning

1. _____ are permeable.

2. Baking soda is a base, while vinegar is an _____.

3. Rubbing your hands together causes _____.

4. A screw uses an _____ to perform work.

5. Potential energy converts to _____ when a book falls off the table.

6. Iron is an _____ that forms rust when combined with oxygen.

7. The lungs are part of the _____.

8. Salt _____ in water, creating a solution.

9. When observers spotted a funnel cloud in the area, a _____ was issued.

10. Plant cells contain a nucleus and _____.

Directions: On your own paper, write a sentence using each term.

11. decomposer   12. abiotic
13. organism   14. mandatory
15. niche   16. dominant
17. scientific method 18. component
19. heterogeneous   20. adaptation

Challenge: Identify five technical terms in the science or social studies text you are currently reading. Use those words to write an original paragraph on your own paper summarizing the topic.

WRITING INFORMATIVE AND EXPLANATORY TEXTS –
Introductions and Conclusions

CCSS.ELA-Literacy.W.7.2f: Provide a concluding statement or section that follows from and supports the information or explanation presented.

Directions: On another piece of paper, write a paragraph using each set of facts. Add an introductory statement and a concluding statement. Use sentence variety and transition words to make your paragraphs interesting and easy to follow.

1. a. First, Thomas Jefferson arranged for the Louisiana Purchase.
    b. Second, he recruited Lewis and Clark to explore the acquisition.
    c. Third, the expedition headed out into the wilderness.

2. a. Plants are producers.
    b. Plants carry out photosynthesis.
    c. Plants have chlorophyll.
    d. Plants make food from sunlight.

3. a. The House of Representatives and Senate are part of the legislative branch.
    b. It is a bicameral legislature.
    c. The job of this branch of government is to make laws.
    d. There are two senators for each state.
    e. The number of representatives depends on the population.

4. a. The circulatory system circulates blood.
    b. Blood carries food and oxygen to the cells.
    c. The heart pumps the blood throughout the body.
    d. Veins and arteries route the blood through the body.

5. a. Water is an important resource.
    b. Water is needed for agriculture.
    c. Water is needed for domestic use.
    d. Water is needed for industry.

Challenge: Write a paragraph about your town or city. Include an introduction, three or four facts, and a conclusion.

Name: _____ Date: _____

WRITING—SECTION THEME: WRITING NARRATIVES

CCSS.ELA-Literacy.W.7.3: Write narratives to develop real or imagined experiences or events using effective technique, relevant descriptive details, and well-structured event sequences.

Story Starts

CCSS.ELA-Literacy.W.7.3a: Engage and orient the reader by establishing a context and point of view and introducing a narrator and/or characters; organize an event sequence that unfolds naturally and logically.

Directions: On another piece of paper, write opening paragraphs for the following stories. Introduce each character and situation in an interesting way.

1. A narrator tells what happened when he and some friends got lost on a hiking trip.

2. A girl and a friend find a peculiar plant in a field next to the school. It brings them extraordinary luck, until something goes wrong.

3. A boy has a fight with his best friend because a mutual acquaintance told a lie.

4. A brother and sister find a bottle on the beach. It has a map inside, which leads them on a treasure hunt.

5. Write an outline of the events that might unfold in one of these stories.

   I. Introduction _____

   _____

   II. First event _____

   _____

   III. Second event _____

   _____

   IV. Third event _____

   _____

   V. A confrontation or disaster _____

   _____

   VI. Conclusion or resolution _____

   _____

Challenge: Write the story you just outlined. Share it with a group of fellow students. Listen to their suggestions. Use their ideas to make improvements in your tale.

Name: _____ Date: _____

WRITING NARRATIVES – Narrative Techniques

CCSS.ELA-Literacy.W.7.3b: Use narrative techniques, such as dialogue, pacing, and description, to develop experiences, events, and/or characters.

Directions: Complete the writing activities below.

1. Write a description of a place you know well. Include details from as many senses as possible.

   _____

   _____

   _____

   _____

   _____

   _____

   _____

2. Write a dialogue between two characters who are disagreeing about something.

   _____

   _____

   _____

   _____

   _____

   _____

   _____

   _____

3. What happened before the scene you just wrote? What happened afterward? Who else was involved?

   _____

   _____

   _____

   _____

   _____

   _____

4. Use your answers to write a short story on your own paper.

Name: _____ Date: _____

WRITING NARRATIVES – Managing Sequence in Narratives

CCSS.ELA-Literacy.W.7.3c: Use a variety of transition words, phrases, and clauses to convey sequence and signal shifts from one time frame or setting to another.

Directions: Write a narrative about what has happened in this class (and just before it) today. Include the sequence signal words at the beginning of each line.

Before _____

_____

_____

When _____

_____

_____

First _____

_____

_____

_____

Next _____

_____

_____

_____

Previously _____

_____

_____

_____

Now _____

_____

_____

_____

_____

_____

Challenge: Use the sequence signal words above to recount any actual or fictitious event. Other sequence terms you may wish to use include: *since, later, then, finally, on Thursday, last July,* and *at 9 A.M.* (or any other specific time).

Name: _____ Date: _____

WRITING NARRATIVES – Stocking a Linguistic Toolkit

CCSS.ELA-Literacy.W.7.3d: Use precise words and phrases, relevant descriptive details, and sensory language to capture the action and convey experiences and events.

Directions: Write a sentence using each word. Use a dictionary if you are uncertain of the word's meaning.

1. disagreement _____

2. exaggerated _____

3. audacity _____

4. autumnal _____

5. betrayal _____

6. broadcaster _____

7. conveniently _____

8. confidential _____

9. dismay _____

10. evict _____

11. far-fetched _____

12. flail _____

13. forfeit _____

14. idolize _____

15. jostle _____

Challenge: Use three or more of your sentences in a story.

Name: _____ Date: _____

WRITING NARRATIVES – Writing Endings

CCSS.ELA-Literacy.W.7.3e: Provide a conclusion that follows from and reflects on the narrated experiences or events.
CCSS.ELA-Literacy.W.7.4: Produce clear and coherent writing in which the development, organization, and style are appropriate to task, purpose, and audience. (Grade-specific expectations for writing types are defined in standards 1–3 above.)

Directions: Write a sentence or two to end a story that includes each set of events.

1. A dog is hiking with his master. The master falls and can't get up. The dog goes for help.

   _____

   _____

   _____

   _____

2. A spider hatches from an egg. She grows, spins a web, and ages. She lays eggs. She dies at the end of the summer.

   _____

   _____

   _____

   _____

3. A girl was stranded on an island after a plane crash. She signals for help. Nothing happens. She is depressed until she makes friends with an orphaned parrot and teaches it to talk.

   _____

   _____

   _____

   _____

4. A wildfire is approaching a mountain valley. A boy tries to get his grandfather to evacuate. The grandfather refuses. He has lived in the house for 70 years and doesn't want to leave.

   _____

   _____

   _____

   _____

Challenge: Choose one of these ideas. Write a short story based upon it. Include an introduction, incidents presented in a logical order, descriptions using sensory details, a conclusion that fits the story, and realistic dialogue. Share your story with other students in your class or group. Use their suggestions to make your tale even better.

WRITING NARRATIVES – Literary Places: Writing a Report

CCSS.ELA-Literacy.W.7.5: With some guidance and support from peers and adults, develop and strengthen writing as needed by planning, revising, editing, rewriting, or trying a new approach, focusing on how well purpose and audience have been addressed. (Editing for conventions should demonstrate command of Language Standards 1–3 up to and including Grade 7 here.)

CCSS.ELA-Literacy.W.7.6: Use technology, including the Internet, to produce and publish writing and link to and cite sources as well as to interact and collaborate with others, including linking to and citing sources.

CCSS.ELA-Literacy.W.7.7: Conduct short research projects to answer a question, drawing on several sources and generating additional related, focused questions for further research and investigation.

CCSS.ELA-Literacy.W.7.8: Gather relevant information from multiple print and digital sources, using search terms effectively; assess the credibility and accuracy of each source; and quote or paraphrase the data and conclusions of others while avoiding plagiarism and following a standard format for citation.

CCSS.ELA-Literacy.W.7.9: Draw evidence from literary or informational texts to support analysis, reflection, and research.

CCSS.ELA-Literacy.W.7.9a: Apply Grade 7 Reading Standards to literature (e.g., "Compare and contrast a fictional portrayal of a time, place, or character and a historical account of the same period as a means of understanding how authors of fiction use or alter history.").

CCSS.ELA-Literacy.W.7.9b: Apply Grade 7 Reading Standards to literary nonfiction (e.g. "Trace and evaluate the argument and specific claims in a text, assessing whether the reasoning is sound and the evidence is relevant and sufficient to support the claims.").

Directions: Write a short research report to answer one of the questions on this page. Use information from several sources, including the library or the Internet. Include a list of the books and websites you consulted. Check the accuracy of facts and quotations.

1. According to Mark Twain, what was life like along the Mississippi River when he was a boy? How does his description compare with life in the same region today?
2. According to Jack London, what was life like in the Klondike when he lived there? How does that compare with life in the same area today?
3. According to John Steinbeck, what was life like in northern California when he lived there? How does that compare with life in the same area today?
4. According to Carl Sandburg, what was life like in Chicago when he lived there? How does that compare to life in Chicago today?
5. According to Robert Frost, what was life like in New England when he lived there? How does that compare to life in New England today?

Challenge: In addition or instead, write a report about the life and works of one of the following authors: Saki, Charles Dickens, William Shakespeare, O. Henry, Edgar Allen Poe, Emily Dickinson, Nathaniel Hawthorne, or Lorraine Hansberry.

Name: _____ Date: _____

SPEAKING AND LISTENING—SECTION THEME: DISCUSSIONS

CCSS.ELA-Literacy.SL.7.1: Engage effectively in a range of collaborative discussions (one-on-one, in groups, and teacher-led) with diverse partners on Grade 7 topics, texts, and issues, building on others' ideas and expressing their own clearly.

Preparing for Discussions

CCSS.ELA-Literacy.SL.7.1a: Come to discussions prepared, having read or researched material under study; explicitly draw on that preparation by referring to evidence on the topic, text, or issue to probe and reflect on ideas under discussion.

Directions: Use the following chart to keep track of facts, opinions, statistics, and controversies as you read. Consult these notes during discussions.

Discussion Preparation Sheet

Topic: _____

Main idea: _____

    Fact: _____

    Fact: _____

    Fact: _____

Expert opinions:

  1. Quote: _____

     Name: _____ Title: _____

     Source: _____

  2. Quote: _____

     Name: _____ Title: _____

     Source: _____

  3. Quote: _____

     Name: _____ Title: _____

     Source: _____

Dates and statistics: _____

_____

Controversies: _____

_____

_____

Other notes: _____

_____

Name: _____ Date: _____

DISCUSSIONS – Discussion Notes

CCSS.ELA-Literacy.SL.7.1b: Follow rules for collegial discussions, track progress toward specific goals and deadlines, and define individual roles as needed.
CCSS.ELA-Literacy.SL.7.1c: Pose questions that elicit elaboration and respond to others' questions and comments with relevant observations and ideas that bring the discussion back on topic as needed.
CCSS.ELA-Literacy.SL.7.1d: Acknowledge new information expressed by others and, when warranted, modify their own views.

Directions: As you are listening to a class discussion, use this form to jot down ideas, questions, and thoughts.

Interesting Questions

1. Speaker: _____
   Question: _____
   _____

2. Speaker: _____
   Question: _____
   _____

3. Speaker: _____
   Question: _____
   _____

4. Speaker: _____
   Question: _____
   _____

5. Speaker: _____
   Question: _____
   _____

My Questions

1. _____
   _____

2. _____
   _____

3. _____
   _____

4. _____

Name: _____ Date: _____

SPEAKING AND LISTENING—SECTION THEME: DIVERSE MEDIA AND FORMATS
Exploring Media

CCSS.ELA-Literacy.SL.7.2: Analyze the main ideas and supporting details presented in diverse media and formats (e.g., visually, quantitatively, orally) and explain how the ideas clarify a topic, text, or issue under study.

Directions: Use this graphic organizer to analyze and compare information from videos, audio presentations, and Internet sites.

Topic: _____

Video

Title: _____

Main idea: _____

    fact: _____

    fact: _____

Advantages of video presentations: _____

_____

Audio

Title: _____

Main idea: _____

    fact: _____

    fact: _____

Advantages of audio presentations: _____

_____

Internet

Title: _____

Main idea: _____

    fact: _____

    fact: _____

Advantages of Internet presentations: _____

_____

Name: _____ Date: _____

DIVERSE MEDIA AND FORMATS – Analyzing a Speech or an Oral Presentation

CCSS.ELA-Literacy.SL.7.3: Delineate a speaker's argument and specific claims, evaluating the soundness of the reasoning and the relevance and sufficiency of the evidence.

Directions: Using the form, take notes on a speech or oral presentation, then answer the questions at the bottom of the page.

Title of the speech or presentation: _____

Speaker: _____

Location: _____

Subject: _____

Speaker's purpose: _____

Main idea: _____

    Example or support: _____

    Example or support: _____

    Example or support: _____

    Example or support: _____

1. Was the speaker convincing? Why or why not? _____

_____

_____

2. Did the speaker rely mainly on facts or emotion? _____

3. How did this emphasis help or hurt the speaker's purpose? _____

_____

_____

4. What was the most memorable part of the speech or presentation? _____

_____

_____

5. What was the least effective part of the speech or presentation? _____

_____

_____

Name: _____   Date: _____

DIVERSE MEDIA AND FORMATS – Creating an Effective Presentation

CCSS.ELA-Literacy.SL.7.4: Present claims and findings, emphasizing salient points in a focused, coherent manner with pertinent descriptions, facts, details, and examples; use appropriate eye contact, adequate volume, and clear pronunciation.
CCSS.ELA-Literacy.SL.7.5: Include multimedia components and visual displays in presentations to clarify claims and findings and emphasize salient points.

Directions: Use this organizer to plan your presentation. Copy the main idea, three supporting points, and facts onto index cards to use during your talk.

Title: _____

Main idea: _____

    Supporting point 1: _____

    Supporting point 2: _____

    Supporting point 3: _____

Introduction: _____

_____

Supporting point 1: (See above) _____

    Fact or detail 1: _____

    Fact or detail 2: _____

    Fact or detail 3: _____

Supporting point 2: _____

    Fact or detail 1: _____

    Fact or detail 2: _____

    Fact or detail 3: _____

Supporting point 3: _____

    Fact or detail 1: _____

    Fact or detail 2: _____

    Fact or detail 3: _____

Conclusion: Restated Main Idea: _____

    Restated point 1: _____

    Restated point 2: _____

    Restated point 3: _____

Quotation or anecdote: _____

_____

Pictures, maps, or other audiovisual aids: _____

_____

Name: _____ Date: _____

DIVERSE MEDIA AND FORMATS – Speaking and Listening Opportunities

CCSS.ELA-Literacy.SL.7.6: Adapt speech to a variety of contexts and tasks, demonstrating command of formal English when indicated or appropriate.

Implement some of these activities for the class as time and resources allow.

1. Arrange panel discussions of books, history, math, or science topics in front of the class.

2. Set up small-group discussions of books, science, or history topics.

3. Encourage students to create electronic slide-show presentations recreating historical events or showing science experiments step by step.

4. Invite students to create narrated electronic slide-show presentations about the time period when a certain novel, short story, or poem was written.

5. Encourage students to present historic speeches in costume or to present recreations of historic characters.

6. Set up an author's day in which each student dresses up as an author and answers questions from the group as that writer might have answered them.

7. Hold a storytelling session in which each student shares a funny, sad, or frightening experience.

8. Arrange a debate about a historic or contemporary issue. Require that students prepare arguments for both sides of the question.

9. Host a poetry reading. Encourage students to present favorite poems to the group. They may perform in duos, small groups, or solo.

10. Invite students to present dramatic monologues or scenes from classic plays.

11. Invite parents, business people from the community, or school staff members to speak about career development or other issues. Encourage students to take notes and ask questions. After the speaker leaves, hold a discussion about the talk.

12. Encourage students to work in pairs or small groups, recording short presentations with a video camera (may use the camera on a laptop, tablet, or cell phone), and then evaluating the results.

13. Arrange for students to listen to or view an historic speech. Then invite them to discuss the historic importance, the speaker's delivery, and the content of the speech.

14. Stage a readers' theater performance of a scene from a play or an adapted novel.

15. Using an audio recorder or a video camera, record a book talk show with a moderator and student guests discussing favorite books from the school or public library. If appropriate, share the finished presentation on the school's keyword-protected website.

Name: _____ Date: _____

LANGUAGE—SECTION THEME: STANDARD ENGLISH GRAMMAR AND USAGE

CCSS.ELA-Literacy.L.7.1: Demonstrate command of the conventions of standard English grammar and usage when writing or speaking.

Phrases and Clauses

CCSS.ELA-Literacy.L.7.1a: Explain the function of phrases and clauses in general and their function in specific sentences.

Directions: Read each sentence. Identify the job of each underlined phrase or clause. Write the correct term from the box on the line.

> **adjective phrase**   **adjective clause**   **clause of comparison**   **adverbial clause**
> **noun clause**   **independent clause**   **adverbial phrase**

1. Glowing lava flowed <u>down the volcano's flank</u>.

   _____

2. The mountains, <u>which rose majestically from the plains</u>, were the Rockies.

   _____

3. <u>When the umpire called the fourth ball</u>, the batter sauntered to first base.

   _____

4. <u>The tsunami inundated the villages</u> on the shore, and it continued a mile inland.

   _____

5. Livestock <u>belonging to an out-of-state rancher</u> were
   threatened.

   _____

6. I found <u>what you lost</u>.

   _____

7. <u>The boy was as tall as the tree his mother planted</u> when he was born.

   _____

Directions: Circle the best choice or choices.

8. Which can stand alone as a sentence?
      a. noun clause   b. independent clause   c. adverbial phrase

9. Which contains a subject and a predicate?
      a. adverbial clause   b. independent clause   c. adverbial phrase

10. Which describes a noun?
      a. adjective phrase   b. adjective clause   c. adverbial clause

Challenge: On a single page in any book, find five examples of clauses or phrases. Identify the function of each one in context. Write the answers on your own paper.

Name: _____ Date: _____

STANDARD ENGLISH GRAMMAR AND USAGE – Simple, Compound, Complex, and Compound-Complex Sentences

CCSS.ELA-Literacy.L.7.1b: Choose among simple, compound, complex, and compound-complex sentences to signal differing relationships among ideas.

Directions: Read the examples. Answer the questions.

Examples:

    a. After an influenza epidemic struck in 1919, many people died.
    b. An influenza epidemic struck in 1919. Many people died.
    c. In 1919, an influenza epidemic struck, and many people died.
    d. An influenza epidemic struck in 1919, and many of the people who became sick died.

1. Which selection is a compound-complex sentence? _____

   Give a reason for your answer. _____

   _____

2. Which selection consists of only simple sentences? _____

   Give a reason for your answer. _____

   _____

3. Which selection is a compound sentence? _____

   Give a reason for your answer. _____

   _____

4. Which selection is a complex sentence? _____

   Give a reason for your answer. _____

   _____

5. Choose the best answer for each question.

   a. Which selection emphasizes that people died as a result of the epidemic? _____

   b. Which selection emphasizes that the epidemic occurred before the deaths? _____

   c. Which selection emphasizes the fact that the epidemic and deaths occurred in 1919?

   _____

   d. Which selection allows the possibility that the epidemic and deaths were not related?

   _____

Challenge: On your own paper, rewrite the following pair of simple sentences as a single compound sentence, a single complex sentence, and a single compound-complex sentence.

Abraham Lincoln was elected in November of 1860. South Carolina seceded from the Union on December 20.

Name: _____ Date: _____

STANDARD ENGLISH GRAMMAR AND USAGE – Using Phrases and Clauses to Build Sentences

CCSS.ELA-Literacy.L.7.1c: Place phrases and clauses within a sentence, recognizing and correcting misplaced and dangling modifiers.*

Directions: Use each set of clauses and phrases to build a sentence.

1. Henry Ford produced the Model T + everyone could own a car + after

   _____

   _____

2. Abraham Lincoln was elected + some southern states decided to secede + as soon as

   _____

   _____

3. honey bees disappear + crops are not pollinated + fruits do not form + when

   _____

   _____

4. fishermen become too efficient + they catch too many fish + when + some aquatic species become endangered + and

   _____

   _____

   _____

5. on the hilltop + the fortress + was impregnable + defenders could see attackers coming + because

   _____

   _____

   _____

6. toward the shed + the mangy dog slunk off + when he spotted the car approaching

   _____

   _____

Directions: On your own paper, use each phrase or clause in a complete sentence.

7. when the team captain scoffed at his throwing ability
8. in a secluded house
9. under the bridge
10. in a white sweater

Challenge: Use one of your sentences in an original short story.

Name: _____ Date: _____

LANGUAGE—SECTION THEME: CAPITALIZATION, PUNCTUATION, AND SPELLING
Proofreading Checklist

CCSS.ELA-Literacy.L.7.2: Demonstrate command of the conventions of standard English capitalization, punctuation, and spelling when writing.

Directions: Answer each of the following questions for your own work or for the work of a fellow student. Place a check mark on the appropriate blank.

Yes　No

_____ _____ 1. Do commas set off all coordinate adjectives, items on a list, or nonrestrictive clauses?

_____ _____ 2. Are there any run-on sentences?

_____ _____ 3. Does every sentence begin with a capital letter?

_____ _____ 4. Are headings capitalized correctly?

_____ _____ 5. Are proper names and titles such as Rep., Rev., and Gov. capitalized?

_____ _____ 6. Are any words capitalized that should not be?

_____ _____ 7. Does every sentence end with an appropriate punctuation mark?

_____ _____ 8. Is each abbreviation followed by a period?

_____ _____ 9. Are all words spelled correctly?

_____ _____ 10. Are quotations and conversations punctuated correctly?

_____ _____ 11. Are a variety of sentence structures used?

_____ _____ 12. Are any ideas or sentences unclear? If yes, which ones?

_____

_____

_____

_____

_____

Challenge: Form a small group of fellow students. Trade copies of a finished essay, report, short story, or poem. Check each other's work for errors. Make suggestions for improvement.

Name: _____ Date: _____

CAPITALIZATION, PUNCTUATION, AND SPELLING – Using Commas to Separate Coordinate Adjectives

CCSS.ELA-Literacy.L.7.2a: Use a comma to separate coordinate adjectives (e.g., *It was a fascinating, enjoyable movie.* but not *He wore an old[,] green shirt.*).

Directions: Follow the instructions for each section.

1. Add commas in the correct places.

   a. A piercing red light was reflected in the eerie vacant rain-slick street.

   b. The tall horticultural specialist wandered among rows of spectacular exotic tropical plants.

   c. The petite new teacher took her place at the worn cluttered desk under the flag.

   d. The ramshackle house on top of the hill huddled behind several mysterious twisted moss-covered cypress trees.

2. Write a sentence using each set of adjectives. Include commas in the correct places.

   a. new orange _____

   _____

   b. mangy grouchy _____

   _____

   c. jovial old _____

   _____

   d. infamous haughty _____

   _____

   e. dainty finicky _____

   _____

   f. fickle young _____

   _____

   g. expansive blue _____

   _____

   h. weary ancient traveler _____

   _____

Challenge: Write a paragraph or short story that includes one of your sentences above.

Name: _____   Date: _____

CAPITALIZATION, PUNCTUATION, AND SPELLING – Spelling Correctly

CCSS.ELA-Literacy.L.7.2b: Spell correctly.

Directions: Circle the misspelled words in each row. Write the correct spellings on the lines provided.

1. evaperate   dissatisfy   dominent   enmity

    _____   _____

2. eardrum   ekosistem   elipticle   emissaries

    _____   _____

3. famished   farce   indorcement   exhonorate

    _____   _____

4. foklore   decimul   convex   courteous

    _____   _____

5. dismay   exhaustive   evikt   feend

    _____   _____

Directions: Circle the word that is spelled correctly. Use it in a sentence.

6. frakshional   fractional   fractionle   fractionul

    _____

    _____

7. conservaytion   conservashion   conservation   consurvation

    _____

    _____

8. hypocrite   hippocrit   hipokrit   hipokrite

    _____

    _____

Challenge: Before typing the final draft of your next report or story, trade papers with a partner. Check each other's spelling carefully. Use a dictionary if you have any questions.

LANGUAGE—SECTION THEME: USING LANGUAGE
Style Evaluation Checklist

CCSS.ELA-Literacy.L.7.3: Use knowledge of language and its conventions when writing, speaking, reading, or listening.

Evaluator's name: _____ Date: _____

Presentation type (circle one):   text   oral   video

Title: _____

Author or presenter: _____

Directions: With 1 being the lowest and 10 being the highest, rate each aspect of the text or presentation.

1.	Clarity of ideas	1 2 3 4 5 6 7 8 9 10
2.	Successful use of repetition	1 2 3 4 5 6 7 8 9 10
3.	Conciseness (not overly wordy)	1 2 3 4 5 6 7 8 9 10
4.	Appropriateness of the language (formal or casual)	1 2 3 4 5 6 7 8 9 10
5.	Effective sentence variety	1 2 3 4 5 6 7 8 9 10
6.	Understandable sentence structure	1 2 3 4 5 6 7 8 9 10
7.	Correct spelling and punctuation (text only)	1 2 3 4 5 6 7 8 9 10
8.	Understandable, confident delivery (oral only)	1 2 3 4 5 6 7 8 9 10

Directions: Write a brief response to each question.

9. What was the most enjoyable part of the text or presentation? Why? _____

_____

_____

_____

10. How could the text or presentation have been improved? _____

_____

_____

_____

Challenge: Share your evaluation in a class discussion. Be prepared to defend your opinions with details and examples.

Name: _____ Date: _____

USING LANGUAGE – Eliminating Wordiness and Redundancy

CCSS.ELA-Literacy.L.7.3a: Choose language that expresses ideas precisely and concisely, recognizing and eliminating wordiness and redundancy.*

Directions: Rewrite each sentence to make it shorter and clearer.

1. When Mom and I left for school, it was this morning, and we were not on time, and Mom was irritable.

   _____

   _____

   _____

2. Before the assault on Pearl Harbor, U.S. specialists had broken the secret diplomatic code the Japanese had created to keep their message a secret, so we knew they were going to attack somewhere, but we didn't know exactly where they were going to attack.

   _____

   _____

   _____

3. Water is essential for life because all living things need water, and living things have to have water to live, and living things cannot live without water because they need it.

   _____

   _____

   _____

4. A decomposer is an organism that is alive, and it breaks down wastes, and it gets rid of dead plants and animals, and it helps to turn dead plants and animals and stuff into soil.

   _____

   _____

   _____

Challenge: Select a sentence from a text. Add extra words, clauses, and phrases. Be careful to preserve the meaning of the sentence. Trade your wordy passage with a partner or with members of a small group. Edit each other's sentences to make them simple and clear. Compare your results with the original sources.

USING LANGUAGE – Building an Effective Vocabulary

CCSS.ELA-Literacy.L.7.4: Determine or clarify the meaning of unknown and multiple-meaning words and phrases based on Grade 7 reading and content, choosing flexibly from a range of strategies.

Directions: When you encounter a new word, record it here. When you fill this page, place it in your notebook and start another one. Find ways to use your collected words in speech and writing as often as possible. Try to add at least one word a day.

Word: _____ Synonym: _____ Antonym: _____
Where found: _____
Sample sentence: _____

Word: _____ Synonym: _____ Antonym: _____
Where found: _____
Sample sentence: _____

Word: _____ Synonym: _____ Antonym: _____
Where found: _____
Sample sentence: _____

Word: _____ Synonym: _____ Antonym: _____
Where found: _____
Sample sentence: _____

Word: _____ Synonym: _____ Antonym: _____
Where found: _____
Sample sentence: _____

Word: _____ Synonym: _____ Antonym: _____
Where found: _____
Sample sentence: _____

Name: _____ Date: _____

USING LANGUAGE – Using Context Clues

CCSS.ELA-Literacy.L.7.4a: Use context (e.g., the overall meaning of a sentence or paragraph; a word's position or function in a sentence) as a clue to the meaning of a word or phrase.

Directions: Read the sentence. Answer the questions.

1. The Great Compromise established a bicameral Congress, instead of a single legislative body, to make laws.

    a. What is the verb in this sentence? _____

    b. What does it mean? _____

    c. To what is the "single legislative body" contrasted? _____

    d. What word does *legislative* describe? _____

    e. What does *bicameral* mean? _____

Directions: Use context clues to define the underlined words.

2. My uncle recited <u>limericks</u>, and by the time he reached the last rhyme, everyone in the room was laughing.

    _____

3. The <u>masqueraders</u> at the carnival revealed their true identities at midnight.

    _____

4. Several <u>miniscule</u> organelles fit within a single plant cell.

    _____

5. Because the speaker mumbled, most of what she said was <u>unintelligible</u>.

    _____

6. A <u>meteorite</u>, actually part of a fractured asteroid, streaked through the sky and exploded over the Arizona desert, creating Meteor Crater.

    _____

7. Because the hermit's cabin was located in a <u>secluded</u> mountain meadow, most people in the region had never seen it.

    _____

8. Near the river's mouth, the muddy waters were <u>languid</u>, lazily easing toward the sea.

    _____

Challenge: On your own paper, write a sentence showing the meaning of one of the following terms: *colony, civilization, artifact, migration, urban, precedent*. Ask a partner to define the word using context clues from your example.

Name: _____　　　Date: _____

USING LANGUAGE – Roots and Affixes

CCSS.ELA-Literacy.L.7.4b: Use common, grade-appropriate Greek or Latin affixes and roots as clues to the meaning of a word (e.g., *belligerent, bellicose, rebel*).

Directions: Choose the best meaning for each underlined root or affix. Write it on the line.

form	wander	grow	foot	run	follow	good	false	hear
toward	self	bad or evil		time	love	people	around	all
law	away from		beyond	fast or speed		make	throw	

1. <u>ab</u>sent _____

2. <u>ad</u>vocate _____

3. <u>ami</u>able _____

4. <u>aud</u>io _____

5. <u>auto</u>matic _____

6. <u>bene</u>ficial _____

7. <u>circum</u>navigate _____

8   ac<u>celer</u>ation _____

9. <u>chron</u>ograph _____

10. in<u>crease</u> _____

11. <u>cur</u>rent _____

12. <u>demo</u>cracy _____

13. <u>err</u>atic _____

14. <u>fact</u>or _____

15. <u>hyper</u>sensitive _____

16. con<u>jec</u>ture _____

17. <u>juris</u>diction _____

18. <u>mal</u>icious _____

19. <u>a</u><u>morph</u>ous _____

20. <u>ped</u>estal _____

21. <u>pan</u>oramic _____

22. <u>pseudo</u>nym _____

23. <u>sequ</u>ential _____

Challenge: On your own paper, use three of the words above in sentences that show their meanings. Choose words that are new to you.

Name: _____ Date: _____

USING LANGUAGE – Pinpointing Meanings, Pronunciations, and Parts of Speech

CCSS.ELA-Literacy.L.7.4c: Consult general and specialized reference materials (e.g., dictionaries, glossaries, thesauruses), both print and digital, to find the pronunciation of a word or determine or clarify its precise meaning or its part of speech.

Directions: Follow the instructions in each section.

1. Write the part of speech of each word.

   a. inoculate _____

   b. isthmus _____

   c. larcenous _____

   d. monologue _____

   e. protuberance _____

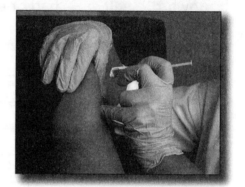

2. Circle the word that rhymes with the underlined word.

   a. <u>raze</u>:   days   cause   says

   b. <u>precarious</u>:   fractious   delicious   hilarious

   c. <u>query</u>:   scullery   dreary   fiery

   d. <u>skew</u>:   so   rue   vie

   e. <u>wield</u>:   yelled   meld   yield

3. Write a synonym or a short meaning for each word

   a. vertex _____

   b. yawl _____

   c. dilate _____

   d. hoax _____

   e. admonish _____

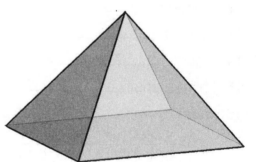

4. Use a thesaurus to find a synonym for each word.

   a. dexterous _____

   b. inequality _____

   c. lucidity _____

   d. aghast _____

   e. ashen _____

Challenge: On your own paper, create riddles based on some of the words on this page. Try them out on fellow students.

USING LANGUAGE – Reading Vocabulary Record Sheet

CCSS.ELA-Literacy.L.7.4d: Verify the preliminary determination of the meaning of a word or phrase (e.g., by checking the inferred meaning in context or in a dictionary).

Directions: As you read, record new words. Write what you think the word means. Later, consult a dictionary and add a synonym or short definition. Practice this technique using the paragraph below.

Practice Passage: The story's **a.** antagonist was as **b.** persuasive as he was **c.** devious. **d.** Indifferent to the harm he was **e.** causing the **f.** inhabitants of his village, he continued his **g.** deceitful campaign to **h.** harass and discredit the town's most honest and competent citizen.

a. word: _____

    guessed meaning: _____

    dictionary meaning: _____

b. word: _____

    guessed meaning: _____

    dictionary meaning: _____

c. word: _____

    guessed meaning: _____

    dictionary meaning: _____

d. word: _____

    guessed meaning: _____

    dictionary meaning: _____

e. word: _____

    guessed meaning: _____

    dictionary meaning: _____

f. word: _____

    guessed meaning: _____

    dictionary meaning: _____

g. word: _____

    guessed meaning: _____

    dictionary meaning: _____

h. word: _____

    guessed meaning: _____

    dictionary meaning: _____

Name: _____ Date: _____

LANGUAGE—SECTION THEME: FIGURATIVE LANGUAGE
Understanding Figurative Language

CCSS.ELA-Literacy.L.7.5: Demonstrate understanding of figurative language, word relation-ships, and nuances in word meanings.

Directions: Follow the instructions in each section.

1. Write the meaning of the underlined phrase.

    a. The first runner took off from the starting blocks <u>like a rocket</u>.

        _____

    b. Lucy claimed <u>you could grill a steak on the sidewalk</u> that afternoon.

        _____

    c. The grizzly was <u>so tall he could reach up and grab a star</u>.

        _____

    d. <u>The lazy sun rested on the horizon for a long time</u> before stretching and rising above the clouds.

        _____

    e. <u>The birds were like an orchestra tuning up</u> outside my window.

        _____

2. Underline the word that fits *best* in each sentence.

    a. My little brother _____ so long we were almost late.

        procrastinated   dawdled   walked   moseyed

    b. The Queen's _____ was elegant and reserved.

        condition   look   demeanor   behavior

    c. Congress was attempting to _____ the country's resources equitably.

        hand out   allocate   spread out   give out

    d. Senator Jones denounced his opponent's _____ comments.

        derogatory   nasty   dirty   horrible

    e. The spy was so brilliant and _____ that nobody suspected him.

        sneaky   tricky   mean   devious

3. Circle the best choice among the synonyms for each use listed.

    a. **conversation:** acquire   get   b. **formal letter:**   test   evaluate

    c. **report:**   choice   alternative   d. **email:**   guess   estimate

Name: _____ Date: _____

FIGURATIVE LANGUAGE – Understanding Literary Allusions

CCSS.ELA-Literacy.L.7.5a: Interpret figures of speech (e.g., literary, biblical, and mythological allusions) in context.

Directions: Write the best biblical or mythological reference on each line. Check a reference source if necessary.

> **Hercules, prodigal son, Narcissus, Mercury, Pandora's box, Lazarus, Pegasus, Scylla and Charybdis, Good Samaritan, Apocalypse, Adonis, David and Goliath, Noah's Ark, snake, Neptune's, Job, Garden of Eden, Zeus, Venus, loaves and fishes**

1. The handsome movie star was a real _____.

2. The new girl in class was a _____ trying to create trouble.

3. You would need the patience of _____ to babysit my little brother.

4. The principal was as calm and dignified as _____, the ruler of Olympus.

5. The submarine was the first to visit _____ realm.

6. My grandmother has so many pets that her house is like _____.

7. Jason was caught between _____ because both choices were equally bad.

8. The poet compared composing to riding _____, a legendary winged horse.

9. Like _____, he couldn't stop admiring himself in the mirror.

10. For men on the ground, the enemy assault seemed like the approach of the _____.

11. Before the arrival of Europeans, the islands were like paradise, a veritable _____.

12. She was as beautiful and fresh as _____, the goddess of love, rising from the sea.

13. When her brother came home, like the _____, he was greeted with a lavish party.

14. The old man was a _____ and allowed the boy to borrow his phone.

15. Everyone contributed so much to the community meal, it was like the _____.

16. Like _____ he rose from the dead.

17. The element _____ was named after the swift messenger of the gods.

18. He was as strong and brave as the ancient hero _____.

19. He opened _____ when he asked the wrong question in the wrong place.

20. The mismatched rivals were like _____, and everyone cheered for the underdog.

Name: _____ Date: _____

FIGURATIVE LANGUAGE – Understanding Word Relationships

CCSS.ELA-Literacy.L.7.5b: Use the relationship between particular words (e.g., synonym/antonym, analogy) to better understand each of the words.

Directions: Follow the instructions in each section.

1. Write the synonym for each word. Choose from the words in the box.

    a. honesty _____

    b. confused _____

    c. force _____

    d. agree _____

    e. face _____

    > concur
    > compel
    > confront
    > bewildered
    > candor

2. Write the antonym for each word. Choose from the words in the box.

    a. conclude _____

    b. include _____

    c. eligible _____

    d. deceitful _____

    e. derogatory _____

    > ineligible
    > complimentary
    > initiate
    > omit
    > candid

3. Write the *best* word from the box in each blank.

    > producer   poisonous   cloud   unbiased   mortified

    a. *Naïve* is to *innocent* as _____ is to *guilty*.

    b. *Acid* is to *base* as *consumer* is to _____.

    c. *Silicon* is to *element* as *cumulus* is to _____.

    d. *Rudimentary* is to *basic* as *toxic* is to _____.

    e. *Copious* is to *plentiful* as *impartial* is to _____.

Challenge: On your own paper, make a list of 10 words. For each word provide a synonym, an antonym, or a word related in some other way such as part/whole, classification/member, or item/quality. Give your list to a partner. Invite your friend to name the relationship between each pair of words.

Name: _____ Date: _____

FIGURATIVE LANGUAGE – Connotations

CCSS.ELA-Literacy.L.7.5c: Distinguish among the connotations (associations) of words with similar denotations (definitions) (e.g., *refined, respectful, polite, diplomatic, condescending*).

Directions: Write each word from the box in the column that best describes its connotation.

eat	lost	devour	misplaced	look	exceptional
odd	glower	condescending		spent	squandered
polite	argument	stench	fragrance	debate	snoop
investigate	unique	weird	miserly	calm	lethargic
economical	curious	confident	egotistical	nosy	mutt
dog	assertive	pushy	naïve	ignorant	obsessed
persistent	rigid	focused	arbitrary	flexible	authoritative
bossy	child	brat	determined	stubborn	intelligent
cunning	steed	nag	chef	cook	cackle
giggle	breeze	gale	smile	smirk	cultured
snobbish	childish	youthful	nostalgic	mushy	arrogant
confident	scrawny	slender	lazy	relaxed	eccentricity
gentle	pushover	peculiar	unique	individuality	

Positive Connotations	Negative Connotations

Challenge: On your own paper, rewrite a magazine advertisement using synonyms for certain descriptive words, changing the meaning of the text. Share the humorous results with classmates.

Name: _____   Date: _____

FIGURATIVE LANGUAGE – Acquiring New Vocabulary

CCSS.ELA-Literacy.L.7.6: Acquire and use accurately grade-appropriate general academic and domain-specific words and phrases; gather vocabulary knowledge when considering a word or phrase important to comprehension or expression.

Directions: Follow the instructions for each section.

1. Choose the *best* word from the box for each sentence. Write it on the line.

> **punctual   bamboozle   perceive   relinquish   treason**

a. The candidate tried to _____ voters into believing a bald-faced lie about his opponent.

b. It was difficult for Kara to _____ care of her beloved horse to the boarding stable, but she couldn't leave him alone while they were gone.

c. The rude man was unable to _____ the effect of his obnoxious behavior on others.

d. Benedict Arnold was a hero during the Revolutionary war but is remembered for his _____, which endangered the cause.

e. Terry tried to be _____, but he was always late.

2. Write a sentence using each word.

a. negligent _____

_____

b. persuasive _____

_____

c. irrelevant _____

_____

d. antagonize _____

_____

e. legendary _____

_____

Challenge: Learn at least one new word a day. Make a point of using it in writing and speech at least five times. At the end of the year, you will have mastered at least 365 new words.

Answer Keys

READING LITERATURE
Story Elements and Inferences (Pg. 1)
1. It is a brooch with a golden stone. She slips it into the yarn basket.
2. Enemies; She doesn't trust them and hides the talisman from them.
3. a friend; He gave her the talisman.
4. the past; the furniture, the room, and the language

Analyzing a Poem (Pg. 2)
1. a seated girl in a red jacket with a mandolin on her lap posing for a painter
2. mandolin, cicada, lyrical, play
3. She sits so still in that jacket of red (model); There's a lyrical tilt to her painted head (painting); It contrasts reality to art.
4. A seventeen-year locust. It sings, which is related to music and poetry. It is a natural thing on the girl's manmade jacket. Other answers are acceptable.

Analyzing a Poem's Structure: The Sonnet (Pg. 3)
1. It demonstrates the form.
2. Five
3. Three
4. at the end
5. weaving a tapestry on a loom; metaphor; It doesn't use *like* or *as.*
6. cloth; because the cloth is really text
Challenge: The couplet summarizes the idea.

Points of View: A Sample Play (Pg. 4)
1. Abby, Jacob, Ryan, Sarah (in that order)
2–3. Responses will vary.

Fiction vs. Nonfiction (Pg. 5)
1. The date the Depression began, how many banks failed, what percentage of people lost jobs
2. The effects of the Depression on ordinary people

3. Most historians and journalists don't write down everything everyone says, and in nonfiction, everything in quotation marks should be accurate (unless noted.)
Challenge: Answers will vary.

READING INFORMATIONAL TEXT
Textual Evidence and Central Ideas (Pg. 6)
1. They monitored the area around Hawaii for the military. The name of the Radio Direction Finder is given, and it says they were on duty.
2. Private Elliot. He wanted more practice.
3. a. Equipment that shows electrical current on a screen.
   b. a spot of light indicating something detected
4. 1941. They are seeing the Japanese planes approaching Pearl Harbor.
5. The Japanese attacked the fleet.

Ideas, Individuals, and Influences (Pg. 7)
1. He was angry and wanted to invade Roman territory.
2. He wanted to keep his word to his father and to avenge his death.
3. He lost too many men and animals.

Using Context Clues (Pg. 8)
1. When flights across the Atlantic became common, it was easier to travel between Europe and America.
2. Without landing or stopping
3. Dangerous, unpredictable, not dependable
4. An early plane with one wing instead of two
5. Financial support
6. Pilot, aviator
7. Famous
8. Bid
9. Stimulating
10. Aircraft, pilots; These historic words lend a period tone to the article.

All About Text Structure (Pg. 9)
1. A. Differentiating Fact from Opinion
   C. 10 Popular Authors
   F. The Importance of Setting in Fiction
2. They do not fit the main idea.
3. Types of Text Structures
4. They help you spot main ideas quickly.
5. Description

Finding the Author's Point of View and the Author's Purpose (Pg. 10)
1. a. third person
   b. first person
   c. second person
   d. third person
   e. first person
2. First person uses *I, my, we,* and *our.* Third person uses *he, she,* and the character's name.
3. a. inform
   b. persuade
   c. entertain
   d. inform
4. How to would include steps and suggestions. (inform) Why would include consequences of not studying. (persuade)
5. a. third person
   b. Inform
   c. many people believe; however, that is not the case

Believe It or Not? Evaluating Claims (Pg. 11)
1. a. punctuality
   b. completing assignments
   c. grades
2. a. It's hard to get up after watching a late-night football game.
   b. No
   c. School is a job, or is more important than football.
3. Humorous, reasons will vary

WRITING—Writing Opinion Pieces
Writing an Opinion (Pg. 12)
Responses will vary.

Clarifying Relationships With Connecting Words and Phrases (Pg. 13)
1. Following, Consequently
2. dilemma is
3. not only — but also
4. To solve this
5. characteristic
6. on the other hand
7. As opposed to
8. For instance
9. In order to
10. finally
11. During
12. similarly

Make It Formal (Pg. 14)
Answers will vary.

Writing Conclusions (Pg. 15)
Answers will vary.

WRITING—Writing Informative and Explanatory Texts
Conveying Ideas and Information (Pg. 16)
Answers will vary.

Using Facts, Definitions, Details, and Quotations (Pg. 17)
Deserts: Facts, Row 1; Definition, Row 2; Details, Row 3; Quotations, Row 1
The Benefits of Physical Activity: Facts, Row 2; Definition, Row 3; Details, Row 1; Quotations, Row 4
Aquifers: Facts, Row 3; Definition, Row 1; Details, Row 4; Quotations, Row 2
Hail: Facts, Row 4; Definition, Row 4; Details, Row 2; Quotations, Row 3

Using Transitions (Pg. 18)
1. one may conclude that
2. Previously
3. as opposed to
4. therefore
5. as well as
6. a.–e. Answers will vary.

Applying Technical Terminology (Pg. 19)
1. Cell membranes
2. acid
3. friction
4. inclined plane
5. kinetic energy
6. element
7. respiratory system
8. dissolves
9. tornado warning
10. organelles
11.–20. Answers will vary.

Introductions and Conclusions (Pg. 20)
Responses will vary.

WRITING—Writing Narratives
Pages 21–26: Responses will vary.

SPEAKING AND LISTENING—
Discussions
Pages 27–28: Responses will vary.

SPEAKING AND LISTENING—Diverse
Media and Formats
Pages 29–31: Responses will vary.

Speaking and Listening Opportunities
(Pg. 32)
Teacher resource page

LANGUAGE—Standard English Grammar
and Usage
Phrases and Clauses (Pg. 33)
1. adverbial phrase
2. adjective clause
3. adverbial clause
4. independent clause
5. adjective phrase
6. noun clause
7. clause of comparison
8. b. independent clause
9. a. adverbial clause
   b. independent clause
10. a. adjective phrase
    b. adjective clause

Simple, Compound, Complex, and
Compound-Complex Sentences (Pg. 34)
1. d, It contains a simple sentence and a complex sentence.
2. b, Each sentence has one subject and one predicate.
3. c, It contains two independent clauses.
4. a, It contains an adverbial clause and an independent clause.
5. a. d;   b. a;   c. c;   d. b

Using Phrases and Clauses to Build
Sentences (Pg. 35)
Answers will vary.

LANGUAGE—Capitalization, Punctuation,
and Spelling
Proofreading Checklist (Pg. 36)
Responses will vary.

Using Commas to Separate Coordinate
Adjectives (Pg. 37)
1. a. eerie, vacant, rain-slick street
   b. spectacular, exotic tropical plants
   c. worn, cluttered desk
   d. several mysterious, twisted moss-covered cypress trees
2. Sentences will vary. Those needing commas are listed:
   b. mangy, grouchy
   d. infamous, haughty
   e. dainty, finicky
   h. weary, ancient traveler

Spelling Correctly (Pg. 38)
1. evaporate, dominant
2. ecosystem, elliptical
3. endorsement, exonerate
4. folklore, decimal
5. evict, fiend
6. fractional
7. conservation
8. hypocrite
(6.–8: Sentences will vary.)

LANGUAGE—Using Language
Style Evaluation Checklist (Pg. 39)
Responses will vary

Eliminating Wordiness and Redundancy
(Pg. 40)
Sentences may vary. Sample answers are given.
1. This morning mom and I left for school late, and mom was irritable.
2. Before the assault on Pearl Harbor, U.S. specialists had broken the Japanese diplomatic code, so we knew they were going to attack in an unknown location.
3. Water is essential for life.
4. A decomposer is a living organism that breaks down dead plants and animals, converting them to soil.

Building an Effective Vocabulary (Pg. 41)
Ongoing student record sheet

Using Context Clues (Pg. 42)
1. a. established
   b. started or made
   c. bicameral Congress
   d. body
   e. two houses or chambers
2. humorous poems
3. party-goers wearing costumes or masks
4. tiny
5. impossible to understand
6. a rock from outer space
7. isolated, hidden
8. unhurried, slow

Roots and Affixes (Pg. 43)
1. away from
2. toward
3. love
4. hear
5. self
6. good
7. around
8. fast or speed
9. time
10. grow
11. run
12. people
13. wander
14. make
15. beyond
16. throw
17. law
18. bad or evil

19. form
20. foot
21. all
22. false
23. follow

Pinpointing Meanings, Pronunciations,
and Parts of Speech (Pg. 44)
1. a. verb
   b. noun
   c. adjective
   d. noun
   e. noun
2. a. days
   b. hilarious
   c. dreary
   d. rue
   e. yield
3. a. point where two sides of an angle intersect
   b. a certain kind of boat
   c. to stretch out or enlarge
   d. ruse, prank, trick
   e. scold, warn
4. a. skillful, adroit, deft
   b. unfairness, discrimination
   c. clarity, reason, logic
   d. horrified, stunned
   e. pale, pallid, pasty

Reading Vocabulary Record Sheet (Pg. 45)
a. antagonist: opponent; villain
b. persuasive: convincing
c. devious: sneaky; deceitful
d. indifferent: uninterested; uncaring
e. causing: creating; producing
f. inhabitants: townspeople
g. deceitful: lying; dishonest
h. harass: bother; annoy

LANGUAGE—Figurative Language
Understanding Figurative Language
(Pg. 46)
1. a. started fast
   b. It was hot outside.
   c. very big bear
   d. sun rose slowly
   e. birds were noisy

2. (Answers may vary; accept reasonable justifications for other choices.)
    a. dawdled
    b. demeanor
    c. allocate
    d. derogatory
    e. devious
3. a. get
    b. evaluate
    c. alternative
    d. guess

Understanding Literary Allusions (Pg. 47)

1. Adonis
2. snake
3. Job
4. Zeus
5. Neptune's
6. Noah's Ark
7. Scylla and Charybdis
8. Pegasus
9. Narcissus
10. Apocalypse
11. Garden of Eden
12. Venus
13. prodigal son
14. Good Samaritan
15. loaves and fishes
16. Lazarus
17. Mercury
18. Hercules
19. Pandora's Box
20. David and Goliath

Understanding Word Relationships (Pg. 48)

1. a. candor   b. bewildered
    c. compel   d. concur
    e. confront
2. a. initiate   b. omit
    c. ineligible   d. candid
    e. complimentary
3. a. mortified   b. producer
    c. cloud   d. poisonous
    e. unbiased

Connotations (Pg. 49)

Positive Connotations:

eat	misplaced
exceptional	look
spent	polite
debate	fragrance
investigate	unique
economical	calm
curious	confident
dog	assertive
naïve	persistent
focused	flexible
authoritative	child
determined	intelligent
steed	chef
giggle	smile
cultured	breeze
youthful	nostalgic
confident	slender
relaxed	individuality
gentle	unique

Negative Connotations:

devour	lost
odd	glower
squandered	condescending
argument	stench
snoop	weird
miserly	lethargic
nosy	egotistical
mutt	pushy
ignorant	obsessed
rigid	arbitrary
bossy	brat
stubborn	cunning
nag	cook
cackle	smirk
snobbish	gale
childish	mushy
arrogant	scrawny
lazy	eccentricity
pushover	peculiar

Acquiring New Vocabulary (Pg. 50)

1. a. bamboozle   b. relinquish
    c. perceive   d. treason
    e. punctual
2. Answers will vary.

Photo Credits for *Common Core Language Arts Workouts: Grade 7*

pg. viii USMC-04473.jpg {PD-USGov/USMC} Slick-o-bot. 7 Dec. 2012. <http://commons.wikimedia.org/wiki/File:USMC-04473.jpg>

pg. 1 Cashmere and silk fingering weight yarn, hand dyed.jpg {PD-CC-SA-3.0} Knittytwins. 12 Oct. 2013. <http://commons.wikimedia.org/wiki/File:Cashmere_and_silk_fingering_weight_yarn,_hand_dyed.jpg>

pg. 2 Mandolin1.jpg {PD-GFDL/CC-SA-3.0} Arent. 10. Aug. 2005. <http://commons.wikimedia.org/wiki/File:Mandolin1.jpg>

pg. 2 Cicada (on hog-plum) (5993624354).jpg {PD-CC-SA-2.0} Bob Peterson. 30 Jul. 2011. <http://commons.wikimedia.org/wiki/File:Cicada_(on_hog-plum)_(5993624354).jpg>

pg. 3 Quill pen.PNG {PD-Author} BWCNY at the English Wikipedia project. Baselmans. 12 Jul. 2007. <http://commons.wikimedia.org/wiki/File:Quill_pen.PNG>

pg. 5 Paul Revere Statue by Cyrus E. Dallin, North End, Boston, MA.JPG {PD-GFDL/CC-SA-3.0} Daderot. 21 Sept. 2005. <http://commons.wikimedia.org/wiki/File:Paul_Revere_Statue_by_Cyrus_E._Dallin,_North_End,_Boston,_MA.JPG>

pg. 7 Hannibal traverse le Rhône Henri Motte 1878.jpg {PD-Old} Henri Motte. 1878. JPS68. 26 May 2011. <http://commons.wikimedia.org/wiki/File:Hannibal_traverse_le_Rhône_Henri_Motte_1878.jpg>

pg. 13 TsunamiHazardZone.jpg {PD-GFDL/CC-SA-3.0} Harriv. Joonasl. 7 Dec. 2005. <http://commons.wikimedia.org/wiki/File:TsunamiHazardZone.jpg>

pg. 15 1765 one penny stamp.jpg {PD-Old/UKGov} United Kingdom Government. 1765. Seewing. 17 Sept. 2010. <http://commons.wikimedia.org/wiki/File:1765_one_penny_stamp.jpg>

pg. 15 Silicon.jpg {PD-CC-SA-3.0} Jurii. 21 Jul. 2009. <http://commons.wikimedia.org/wiki/File:Silicon.jpg>

pg. 15 Aiga nosmoking inv.svg {PD-USDOT/AIGA} AIGA. Thadius856. 9 Jan. 2008. <http://commons.wikimedia.org/wiki/File:Aiga_nosmoking_inv.svg>

pg. 18 Corn field in San Bartolo.jpg {PD-CC-SA-3.0} Elizabeth Sampson. 29 Jun. 2009. <http://commons.wikimedia.org/wiki/File:Corn_field_in_San_Bartolo.jpg>

pg. 19 Allium-Differenzierung03-DM100x HF ba1.jpg {PD-CC-SA-3.0} Dr. phil.nat Thomas Geier. Martin Bahmann. 20 Oct. 2009. <http://commons.wikimedia.org/wiki/File:Allium-Differenzierung03-DM100x_HF_ba1.jpg>

pg. 20 USCapitol.jpg {PD-CC-SA-2.5} F. Malotaux. Zarex. 24 Jan. 2007. <http://commons.wikimedia.org/wiki/File:USCapitol.jpg>

pg. 24 Toolbox (226362564).jpg {PD-CC-SA-2.0} Daren. 27 Aug. 2006. <http://commons.wikimedia.org/wiki/File:Toolbox_(226362564).jpg>

pg. 25 On the trails with the dog (7018780019).jpg {PD-CC-SA-2.0} vastateparkstaff. 19 Mar. 2012. <http://commons.wikimedia.org/wiki/File:On_the_trails_with_the_dog_(7018780019).jpg>

pg. 33 Pitcher and batter in youth league.jpg {PD-CC-SA-2.0} Kathy. 20 Apr. 2008. <http://commons.wikimedia.org/wiki/File:Pitcher_and_batter_in_youth_league.jpg>

pg. 34 SpanishFluPosterAlberta.jpg {PD-Old} Provisional Board of Health, Alberta. ca 1918. Infrogmation. 28 Apr. 2009. <http://commons.wikimedia.org/wiki/File:SpanishFluPosterAlberta.jpg>

pg. 35 Tammerkoski hameensilta under the bridge drained.JPG {PD-Free Art License 1.3} Eero Yli-Vakkuri. 20 Aug. 2011. <http://commons.wikimedia.org/wiki/File:Tammerkoski_hameensilta_under_the_bridge_drained.JPG>

pg. 37 Tropical Palm House, Royal Botanic Garden, Edinburgh. - geograph.org.uk - 1475464.jpg {PD-CC-SA-2.0} Ian Petticrew. 8 Aug. 2009. <http://commons.wikimedia.org/wiki/File:Tropical_Palm_House,_Royal_Botanic_Garden,_Edinburgh._-_geograph.org.uk_-_1475464.jpg>

pg. 40 Attack on Pearl Harbor Japanese planes view.jpg {PD-Old/USGov} Taken from a Japanese plane. 7 Dec. 1941. W.wolny. 10 Oct. 2005. <http://commons.wikimedia.org/wiki/File:Attack_on_Pearl_Harbor_Japanese_planes_view.jpg>

pg. 43 Hear Music touchscreen.jpg {PD-CC-SA-2.0} Thomas Duesing. 12 Aug. 2005. <http://commons.wikimedia.org/wiki/File:Hear_Music_touchscreen.jpg>

pg. 43 Speeding Car-140mpg.jpg {PD-GFDL/CC-SA-3.0} Tom Corser www.tomcorser.com. 2009. <http://commons.wikimedia.org/wiki/File:Speeding_Car-140mph.jpg>

pg. 44 Nurse administers a vaccine.jpg {PD-Author/NIH} Rhoda Baer, National Cancer Institute, National Institutes of Health. 21 Sept. 2009. <http://commons.wikimedia.org/wiki/File:Nurse_administers_a_vaccine.jpg>

pg. 44 Square pyramid1.png {PD-CC-SA-3.0} A2569875. 23 Jun. 2014. <http://www.commons.wikimedia.org/wiki/File:Square_pyrmid1.png>

pg. 46 US Navy 111004-N-KT462-097 Aviation Maintenance Administrationman 3rd Class Jackie Wilson trains for the Armed Forces Track and Field team while de.jpg {PD-USGov/Navy} Mass Communication Specialist 2nd class Jon Dasbach. 4 Oct. 2011. <http://commons.wikimedia.org/wiki/File: US_Navy_111004-N-KT462-097_Aviation_Maintenance_Administrationman_3rd_Class_Jackie_Wilson_trains_for_the_Armed_Forces_Track_and_Field_team_while_de.jpg>

pg. 48 Kitchen bleach.JPG {PD-GFDL/CC-SA-3.0} Mk2010. 8 Feb. 2011. <http://commons.wikimedia.org/wiki/File:Kitchen_bleach.JPG>

pg. 48 Juicing the lemons (6027988479).jpg {PD-CC-SA-2.0} Leslie Seaton. 20 Jul. 2011. <http://commons.wikimedia.org/wiki/File:Juicing_the_lemons_(6027988479).jpg>

pg. 50 Pferdestall 1058.jpg {PD-GFDL/CC-SA-3.0} Moros. 24 Feb. 2008. <http://commons.wikimedia.org/wiki/File:Pferdestall_1058.jpg>